Thomas Alva Edison

Thomas Alva Edison

Miracle Maker

by Mervyn D. Kaufman

illustrated by Cary

A Yearling Book

This book is for
Mary Harbage, who began it all.

Published by
DELL PUBLISHING CO., INC.
1 Dag Hammarskjold Plaza
New York, N.Y. 10017

Copyright © 1962 by Mervyn D. Kaufman

Reprinted by arrangement with Garrard Publishing Co.
ISBN:0-440-48813-3
Printed in U.S.A.
Sixth Dell Printing—September 1979

THOMAS ALVA EDISON is one of the *Discovery* biographies
published by Garrard Publishing Co., Champaign, Illinois.
Discovery books are published by Garrard in library bindings.

This book is one of a series of educational, informative
biographies, presented in a lively, colorful and interesting
manner. They are designed and edited so that they can be
read and enjoyed by young readers through the elementary
grades. All facts are authentic for they have been carefully
checked with leading sources for historical accuracy.

Contents

Chapter *1*

Always Experimenting

BANG!

The sound shook the Edison house in Port Huron, Michigan. Samuel Edison looked up from his newspaper. His wife, Nancy, was making a cake in the kitchen. She put down her spoon and started for the cellar door.

"Is that Al down there?" Mr. Edison called from the next room.

"Yes, dear," Mrs. Edison replied. "He's doing things with those chemicals again."

"One of these days that boy will blow us all to smithereens," Mr. Edison said.

"Oh, he'll be careful. Al knows what he's doing in his laboratory," Mrs. Edison said. Then she opened the cellar door.

"Al, are you all right?" she called. "What was it this time?"

"Just another experiment, Ma," he cried. "I mixed two chemicals to see if they would explode. And they did!" He was sweeping up pieces of broken glass. The explosion had burst a large glass jar.

"Well, you'd better be at your chores now. Supper will be ready soon," she said.

"Yes, Ma. I'll be right up."

Al was glad his laboratory was in the cellar now, instead of upstairs in his bedroom. He had a big work table here. Two wooden shelves hung from the wall above it. They held little bottles filled with powders and liquids of many colors. These were chemicals. Each time Al tried a new experiment, he learned something new about science and chemicals.

Al walked into the kitchen a few minutes later. He carried some wood for the stove.

"Thomas Alva Edison, you *are* a sight!" his mother said.

And he certainly was. His face was dirty. His shirt was spotted from a yellow chemical he had spilled. His pants were torn.

He set down the wood and went out to the back yard. There he began to fill the oil lamps that lighted the house each night.

"What's to become of that boy, Sam?" Mrs. Edison asked her husband. "He's either reading or playing with those chemicals. He's only ten. He should play outdoors more with his friends. I think he stays in the house too much."

"Maybe we should send him back to school," Mr. Edison said.

"No," she said, with a firm shake of her head. "Not the Port Huron school. He can learn better right here."

Al had gone to the Port Huron school for a while. That was when his family first moved to town, in 1855. But Al did not get along with his teacher.

He was always asking questions. "Where does the wind come from?" "Why does water run downhill?"

Al asked so many questions that his teacher said he was a "bother." So his mother took him out of school.

"I taught school once," she said proudly. "I can teach Al his lessons." From that time on, she did. There were fewer schools in those days. Many children did their lessons at home.

One thing Mrs. Edison could not teach her son was how to save money. Every penny he earned from doing chores was spent on his laboratory. Still, he never had enough money to buy all the chemicals he wanted.

"How can I earn more money?" He thought and thought.

One day his father had an idea. "Why don't you grow vegetables in our back yard? Then you can sell them."

Al and a friend dug a garden. They planted lettuce, corn, tomatoes and cabbage. Soon the vegetables were ready to pick. The boys put them in big baskets to sell. They hired a horse and wagon and rode along the streets of Port Huron.

"Sweeeeet corn . . . nice, big, ripe tomaaaaaytoes," they called. The people came out of their houses to buy.

As the months passed, Al grew tired of selling vegetables. It took too much time for the money he earned. There *had* to be another way to earn money for more chemicals.

"I'll find a way, somehow," he said.

Chapter 2

"Something Snapped"

It was a cold November morning in 1859. Al stood by the new railroad station in Port Huron. A large crowd stood with him. Everyone wanted to see the train leave the station. It was the first train to go from Port Huron to Detroit. The trip would take three hours.

Al looked at the shiny new cars.

"I'm going to ride in one of those cars some day," he said to himself. Just then three men came up behind him.

Al could hear them talking. One of them said he wished he could find a boy to sell candy and newspapers on the train.

Al turned around. "Did you say you were looking for a boy?" he asked.

"Why, yes, son," said the tallest man. "Would you like the job?"

"Yes. Yes, *sir*," Al said. His eyes were wide with excitement.

"How old are you?" asked the man.

"Twelve," said Al.

"Well, you'd better talk with your folks first. Tell them you'll be home every night. If they say it's all right, be here early tomorrow." Al ran home at once to talk with his parents.

Mrs. Edison did not like the idea at first.

"The job may be good for him, Nancy," Mr. Edison told her. "It's time he got to see what a big city is like."

Finally Mrs. Edison agreed. So the next morning Al was at the station bright and early. He went to work as soon as the train started.

He hurried through the cars, crying, "Candy, apples, newspapers, sandwiches." Later, when he was not busy, he did his lessons. He sat in the baggage car and read. Science books were his favorites.

Soon Al was earning enough money to pay for his chemicals. He had enough left over to give his mother seven dollars every week. It was not long before he found a way to earn even *more* money.

Coming back from Detroit, Al carried more newspapers than he could sell on the train. He sold the extra papers to people waiting at stations along the way. Soon Al had many new customers.

He was the first person off the train each time it stopped. He was almost always the last to get on before it started again.

One night he stayed on the platform too long. The train started to leave without him. He had to *race* to reach it. He grabbed the railing at the side of the baggage car. He was strong, but he could not swing himself up.

Al held on, but his feet were dragging on the ground. He did not dare let go. He knew he might be crushed by the wheels.

Someone on the train saw Al and called to a brakeman. "Help that boy. He may be killed!"

The brakeman reached out, grabbed Al by the ears and pulled him aboard.

"Thanks. You saved my life," Al said. His voice was very weak.

"That's all right, son," said the brakeman. "I hope I didn't hurt your ears. They were the only things I could catch hold of." Al smiled and shook the brakeman's hand. His ears were ringing loudly. Soon they began to ache.

He did not tell his parents what had happened. But they soon noticed that something was wrong with his hearing.

"Al, I want you to take a day off," Mrs. Edison said. "I think Dr. Marshall should look at your ears."

Al told the doctor what had happened on the train. "When the brakeman grabbed my ears," he said, "something snapped inside my head."

Dr. Marshall looked Al over carefully. Finally he said, "Al, I'm afraid there's nothing I can do to help you. Your hearing will get worse as you get older. Some day you may not hear at all."

Mrs. Edison said very little on the way home. Even Mr. Edison was quiet when he heard the bad news. But Al did not seem to mind.

"There's so much I want to see and do," he said cheerfully. "I can't worry about being deaf. Anyway, it won't happen for a long, long time."

Chapter 3

Dots and Dashes

"Hello, Jim."

Al tapped out this greeting in dots and dashes on his telegraph. He had a sending and receiving set in the cellar. His friend Jim Clancy had one too.

The boys had put up wire between their houses. Telegraph signals went along the wire. Every night Jim and Al spent many hours sending messages. The dots and dashes were part of the Morse code.

It was late. Mr. and Mrs. Edison returned from a visit with friends. They could hear the sound of the telegraph coming from the cellar.

"That boy should be in bed by now," Mrs. Edison said. "He has to be up by six."

Mr. Edison opened the cellar door. "It's past your bedtime, Al," he called. "You're a working man, remember?"

"Yes, Pa. I'll be right up." Sighing, Al tapped out "Good night."

"Bedtime. What a waste!" he thought. "I wish I could make Pa *want* me to stay up late." Then he had an idea.

The next night Al came home without a Detroit newspaper for his father.

"Where is my paper?" Mr. Edison asked.

"Oh," said Al, "I guess I left it at Jim's house." Mr. Edison was disappointed. Like most people, he was worried about the country. The year was 1860. That was one year before the Civil War began.

After supper, Mr. Edison sat down to read. Al watched him out of the corner of an eye. He could see that his father was not enjoying the book.

"Pa," he said, "maybe we can get the news after all."

"How?" his father asked. "It's too late for you to be running down to Jim's place."

"Why couldn't Jim send the news by telegraph?" Al asked.

"That would take all night," said Mr. Edison.

"Jim is not as fast as I am," Al said proudly. "But he *is* pretty good."

"Well," said Mr. Edison slowly, "let's try it."

Al and his father went down to the cellar. Al sent a message to Jim. Soon the telegraph was clicking away. Al turned the dots and dashes into words for his father to read.

For the next two nights Al "forgot" to bring home a newspaper. He and his father sat up late listening to the telegraph.

Finally Mr. Edison caught on. "I see through your tricks," he said, laughing. "You bring me the newspaper. From now on, I'll let you stay up until half-past twelve to practice on your telegraph."

Al was happy with the bargain he made. The next day he was even happier. He asked Conductor Stevenson if he could put his laboratory on the train. To his surprise, Mr. Stevenson said "yes."

So Al moved his belongings into the baggage car. He was the proud owner of the world's first traveling laboratory.

Chapter 4

Turning Point

One day Al saw a sign in the window of a store in Detroit.

"For sale," it said. "One small, used printing press in good condition."

Al's eyes danced with excitement. He went into the shop and bought the old press.

"What do you want it for?" the shopkeeper asked.

"I'm going to start a newspaper," Al said. He carried the printing press back to the train.

He taught himself to run the press. Soon he was printing the first copies of his newspaper. He called it *The Weekly Herald*.

The paper had jokes and poems. It had stories about people who lived in towns along the railroad. Al printed only a few papers at first. But soon he was selling over 400 copies each week.

He was so busy now that he had little time to play with his friends. But he did take time off each day when the train stopped at Mt. Clemens. That was where it picked up freight cars.

Sometimes an hour passed before the train was ready to go again. This was time enough for Al to walk around a bit. He liked to talk to the stationmaster, Mr. Mackenzie.

One day Mr. Mackenzie was busy sending a telegraph message. So Al waited outside the station house. He watched as an engine pushed a string of freight cars along the track. The moving cars bumped into one that was standing still. It rolled along by itself, picking up speed.

Just then the little Mackenzie boy, Jimmy, ran onto the railroad track to pick up some pebbles. He did not see the freight car coming toward him. But Al did!

He raced to the track and grabbed the boy. The two of them fell to the other side of the track. The freight car rolled by without hurting them.

Mr. Mackenzie rushed from his office. "How can I thank you?" he cried.

"You saved my son's life. I must do something for you in return."

"No, no," Al said, "you don't have to . . ."

"*I* know," said Mr. Mackenzie suddenly. "I could teach you to be a railroad telegraph operator. How would you like that?"

"Well . . ." Al said. "I guess I would like that fine."

"Then it's a bargain," said Mr. Mackenzie. "You hire a boy to do your work between here and Detroit. Then you can get off here every day. We can work until the train comes back again. Learn what I can teach you. Then you'll be ready to get a *real* job."

Al and Mr. Mackenzie started working together the very next day.

Railroad signals were not the same as Morse code. But Al learned the signals easily.

Now he was busier than ever. His friends helped him with his job and with his newspaper. He still found time to study and work in his traveling laboratory.

One day he was doing an experiment. The train gave a sudden jerk. A dangerous chemical fell on the floor and caught fire. Clouds of gray smoke filled the baggage car.

Al was frightened. He pulled off his coat and tried to beat out the flames with it. The fire got bigger instead of smaller. Al was nearly burned.

"Help! Fire!" he shouted as loudly as he could.

Conductor Stevenson heard him and ran into the car. He picked up a pail of sand and poured it on the flames. Then he poured on a pail of water. The sand and water were there in case of fire. Al had been too frightened to remember them.

The fire finally went out. It left a big, black hole in the floor.

Al said he was sorry. But the conductor was very angry. He told Al to get off the train at the very next stop. When the train slowed down, he pushed Al out the door.

"Wait," Al cried. "My things are still in there!"

"Here they are," Mr. Stevenson called. He tossed all of Al's belongings out of the car. Everything was ruined.

The train rolled on into the night. Al was alone. It was late. He was hungry and very tired.

"This is the end," he thought. "I'll never amount to anything now."

It was a night he would never forget. But it was not "the end," only a turning point.

The Civil War was being fought. The telegraph operator in Port Huron left his job and joined the army. Al was given the job. His hearing was getting worse. But he could still hear the clickety-clacks of the telegraph. Soon he became known as one of the fastest telegraph operators in the country.

Chapter 5

The First Invention

"Mother . . . Father!"

Al burst into the Edison dining room. He was out of breath.

"You're late, son," Mrs. Edison said. "We started supper without you."

"Ma," he said, still puffing. "I've left my job. But I've got a new one, a better one. I have to leave tomorrow."

"What kind of job, Al?" Mr. Edison asked.

"I'm going to work for the railroad again. But this time I'm going to be a telegraph operator—in Stratford."

"Stratford," said Mrs. Edison. "But that's 75 miles away."

"You're only seventeen, son," Mr. Edison said. "Your mother and I hate to see you leave home so soon."

"I know, Pa," said Al. "But . . ."

"*But* if you think this is a good job and you want it, go ahead," Mr. Edison said. He looked at his wife. She nodded. Then she smiled.

"Well, son," she said, "we'd better start packing your clothes."

Al got out his trunk. He packed so many books in it that he barely had room for clothes. He had to sit on the trunk to get the lid closed and locked.

He and his father carried it downstairs. It was almost too heavy for them.

The next day Al left for his first job away from home. During the next five years he had many jobs in many cities. He earned a lot of money as a telegraph operator. But he spent nearly all of it on more equipment for experiments.

Finally Al came to New York City. He was twenty-two years old. He had forty-two cents in his pocket.

Al had a friend in New York. His name was Frank Pope. Frank worked for the Gold Indicator Company. In those days the price of gold changed many times each day. The Gold Indicator Company let businessmen know whenever the price changed. The news was sent out over telegraph wires.

Al went to the Gold Indicator Company to find his friend, Frank. Just as he got there, the telegraph machine broke down. No one at the company knew how to fix it.

Al spotted the trouble right away. He took off his coat and went to work. Soon the big machine was running again.

The head of the company was pleased. He offered Al a job. He said Al could look after all the machinery in the building.

"It's a hard job," Al told his friend, Frank. "I hope it doesn't take too much time. I want to work on my invention."

"What kind of invention?" Frank asked.

"A stock ticker," said Al.

"You're too late, Al," said Frank. "Somebody has already invented one."

"I know," said Al. "But that one doesn't work very well. Mine will be better. You'll see."

A stock ticker was a special kind of telegraph. It was used in offices where stocks were sold. Stocks are shares of big companies that people own. News about the price of the stocks came over a telegraph wire. The stock ticker printed the news on long strips of paper.

Al's machine *was* better. It worked faster than other stock tickers. And it printed clearer. It was so good that an important businessman wanted to buy it.

"What do you think your invention is worth?" the man asked Al.

44

Al did not know what to say. He had worked hard on his invention. He wanted to ask five thousand dollars for it. Then he decided to ask only three thousand.

At last he said, "Why don't you make an offer?"

"Very well," the businessman said. "How about forty thousand dollars?"

"That sounds fair enough," said Al. His voice trembled. He had never been so happy!

Forty thousand dollars! Why, that was enough money to buy things for more inventions. It was enough to rent a place to work. Enough to hire some men to help him.

He could send some money home to his parents too. They were getting older.

They needed the help he could give them.

Al left the businessman's office in a kind of dream. The telegraph operator from Port Huron, Michigan, was now an inventor in New York.

Chapter 6

Talking Tinfoil

Thomas Alva Edison's first laboratory was in Newark, New Jersey. There he worked on many inventions. He hired many men to help him. He even hired a young girl. She helped out in the office. Her name was Mary Stilwell.

She did not work in the office very long. On Christmas Day, 1871, she and the inventor were married. She called him Thomas, as most people did now.

In a few years the Edisons had three children. The oldest was Marion. They nicknamed her "Dot." Thomas Jr. was nicknamed "Dash." The youngest boy was called William Leslie.

Edison loved playing with his children. But he could not be with them very often. He worked hard in his laboratory. He often came home after the children were in bed.

In 1876 Edison built a big, new laboratory. It was in Menlo Park, New Jersey. The Edison family moved into a house near the laboratory. There was a wide, green lawn where the children could play.

Soon Edison was working on an important new invention. It was a machine that he hoped would talk.

"Talk!" cried one of his helpers. "How can a machine *say* anything?"

"Just wait," the inventor said with a smile. "One of these days I'll show you that it can be done."

It was not long before Edison was ready to try out his new machine.

"Bring me some tinfoil," he called to one of his helpers. The man brought some thin sheets of the shiny metal. The other men stopped their work and came to watch.

A strange looking little machine sat on the table in front of Edison. The men watched as he wrapped a sheet of tinfoil around a part of the machine. This part was fairly long and shaped like a tube.

Then Edison started turning a crank.

The tube wrapped in tinfoil turned round and round. Then Edison bent over the little machine. He shouted as loud as he could.

>*"Mary had a little lamb.*
>*Its fleece was white as snow.*
>*And everywhere that Mary went,*
>*The lamb was sure to go."*

Edison stopped cranking. He turned the machine back to the starting point. His helpers were laughing now. It was funny to hear Mr. Edison saying that old nursery rhyme.

The inventor turned the crank again. The tube began to spin round and round.

Suddenly the men stopped laughing. The sound of Edison's voice was coming from the tinfoil.

"Mary had a little lamb.

Its fleece was white as snow . . ."

These were the first words ever recorded. Edison was right. He *had* made a machine that could talk. It was the phonograph. It became one of his most famous inventions.

Chapter 7

A Safe, Bright Light

Thomas Edison sat in his laboratory. His feet rested on his desk. It was nearly midnight, an October night in 1879. Edison was tired and worried. He had been working on one invention for over a year. He began it soon after he had finished the phonograph.

He was trying to invent a new kind of light. He wanted one that would burn brighter than the gas lights everyone used.

Gas lights flickered like candle light. And there was always a danger of fire. Edison wanted a light that would be steady and even. And he wanted it to be safer and cleaner than gas light.

"Electricity is the answer," he said. "But how?" The problem had bothered him for a long time.

"To make light, something has to burn or glow," he thought. "There's nothing hard about that."

He looked at the lights in the laboratory. A wick burned in the candle on the desk. Gas burned in the lamps overhead.

"What can I burn in my *electric* lamps?" he wondered. "It must be something that will glow for a long time. It's no use if it burns right up."

So far, only one thing was certain. An electric light would have to burn inside a glass bulb. The bulb must be sealed tightly so no air could get in. Even a tiny bit of air would make the light go out.

Edison smiled. He remembered the many things he had tested inside glass bulbs. First there was a piece of horsehair, then straw, then cornsilk and then a splinter of wood. He had even used a hair from the beard of one of his helpers!

Nothing had worked when the electricity was turned on. Everything he tested had either broken apart or burned right up.

The tired inventor leaned back in his chair and closed his eyes for a moment.

His fingers toyed with some cotton thread that lay on his desk. Suddenly he had an idea.

He did not go home at all that night. Instead, he slept right at his desk. He was up at dawn.

"Mr. Edison, you're here early again," one of his assistants said.

"No," said the inventor, rubbing his eyes. "Let's just say that I stayed late. There's something I want to try."

Edison found some small pieces of cotton thread. He rolled them in lampblack. This was a black material that felt like soft tar.

Edison carefully bent the blackened threads into the shape of hairpins. Then he set each of them into a small clay dish.

"Here," he called to his assistant. "Bake these in the furnace so they'll get hard. Some of the threads may break. But I hope one will come out strong enough for us to use."

Several hours later, the threads were taken out of the furnace. Edison chose one that looked very strong. He put it inside a glass bulb.

"All set," he said. "Turn on the electricity." An assistant pulled the switch. The bulb glowed brightly. It did not flicker. The men in the laboratory crowded around Edison's work table.

"Let's not get excited, boys," Edison warned. "This one will probably burn up just as the others did."

Edison and his men watched the lamp.

Minute after minute it glowed brightly. Then hour after hour. Then, late the next day, it went out. It had burned for forty hours!

Two months later, curious people from many towns visited Menlo Park. They came to see the Edison lamps.

What a sight greeted them as they stepped off the train! Electric lamps burned brightly on the streets that led to the laboratory. To the visitors the sight seemed like a miracle. To the inventor and his helpers, it was the end of much hard work.

Chapter 8

Light for the City

"Imagine us being *here*!" Thomas Edison told his assistants.

They stood outside a large building in New York City. "Why, when I first came to this city, I hadn't enough money to rent a room. Now I've got a whole building!"

Edison and his men had come to New York to set up an electric power system. They hoped it would provide enough electricity to light up a part of the city.

They brought several small machines with them. These were generators. The generators made electric power for lamps in the Edison building.

Soon there were lights from every window. People stopped their horse-drawn carriages to look. The lights burned brightly and steadily. Everyone knew that Thomas Edison was in town.

First, the inventor and his men built several *large* generators. A lot of power would be needed to light up even a small part of the city.

Then workmen got busy with shovels and picks. They dug deep trenches in the hard earth below the city streets. Fourteen miles of wire were laid into these trenches. The wires connected each building to a generator.

Setting up a power system was not an easy job. It took a year and a half. In September, 1882, the job was finished.

A small group of men stood around Edison inside the power house. The big moment had come. Would his idea work?

The inventor took a deep breath, closed his eyes, and pulled a switch. The electric lights flashed on.

"Very good, very good!" said a man from a New York newspaper.

"Sir," said Edison, "this is only the beginning!" And Edison was right. It was not long until Edison lamps were lighting up cities all over the world.

Chapter 9

Glenmont

The Edisons took a vacation. It was the first time in a long while that Thomas could have fun with his children.

These were happy days. But the happiness did not last. Mrs. Edison became sick.

Thomas had to go to New York to see how the power system was working. One night he got a message. "Mrs. Edison is worse," the message said. "You'd better come home."

The inventor returned to Menlo Park. His wife died a short time later. Thomas was so sad that he closed up the house and laboratory. He sent the children to live with Grandmother Stilwell. Then he moved back to New York.

Edison's friends tried to cheer him up. One family invited him often to their home in Boston. There he met young Mina Miller of Akron, Ohio. She liked hearing Edison talk about his exciting work.

Mina even learned the Morse code. One night Thomas took her hand. He tapped a message in Morse code with his fingers.

"Will you marry me?" the message said.

"Yes," she replied, tapping his hand with her fingers. Soon they were married. They went to Florida on their honeymoon.

When they returned, the whole Edison family moved to West Orange, New Jersey. Their new house was called Glenmont. Its many windows looked out over a wide, green valley.

"Some day," Edison said, "my laboratory will *cover* that valley."

Edison was right. The laboratory at West Orange grew and grew. Soon it was ten times bigger than the one at Menlo Park.

Glenmont was Edison's home for the rest of his life. The laboratory at West Orange was where he made some of his most important inventions.

Chapter 10

The "Black Maria"

In 1889, Mina and Thomas Edison came home from a trip to Europe. They had met many famous inventors there. They had also met Kings and Queens.

"Welcome home!" cried one of Edison's assistants.

"It's good to be back," the inventor said, sniffing the cool autumn air. "Tell me, have you been working hard?"

"Yes, sir," said the assistant. "We've been following all your directions."

"And?" Edison asked.

"And we have something to show you," said the man. He smiled broadly.

Later, Edison went into a building where "secret" work had been going on for many months. One of his helpers showed him to a seat in front of a large, white screen.

"Mr. Dickson, it's good to see you," said Edison. Mr. Dickson smiled and turned off the light. Then he turned on a large machine at the back of the room. It looked like a funny kind of lantern. Next to it was a phonograph.

Mr. Dickson turned a crank on the machine. A beam of light flashed across the room and onto the screen. Then a picture of Mr. Dickson flickered on the screen.

The man in the picture moved. He raised his hat and smiled. From the phonograph came the words, "Good morning, Mr. Edison. Glad to have you back." It was Mr. Dickson's voice.

Edison laughed with pleasure. He was seeing the very first motion picture. His newest invention worked!

Soon workmen were busy putting up a new building at the Edison laboratory. This one was different from the others. It was long and thin and was covered with black tar paper.

The building was nicknamed "Black Maria." It looked very much like the police wagons people then called Black Marias.

One day Edison saw some children looking at the new building.

"We make our movies there," he told them. He pointed out the Black Maria's special roof. Part of it could be raised to let in sunlight. Or it could be lowered to make the inside very dark.

"See," Edison said. "The roof is up now. That means the men need light for the picture they are making."

"But Mr. Edison," one boy said, "the sun is going down. There isn't much light."

"Maybe the building should be turned to face the sun," another boy said with a laugh.

"No sooner said than done, my lad," said Edison. "Watch."

Just then, workmen began to push at the side of the Black Maria. Slowly it turned.

"See," said Edison. "It's built so we can swing it around. We can follow the sun from morning to night."

People liked to visit the Edison laboratory. They liked to see movies being made. So did Edison. But he had no idea how popular his invention would become. He never dreamed that movies would grow to be one of the biggest businesses in the world.

Chapter *11*

Golden Jubilee

"All aboard, Mr. Edison!" cried the railroad conductor. He took the old inventor by the arm and helped him on the special train. Mrs. Edison got on too.

Thomas Edison slowly went to his seat. He was 82 now. His white hair looked like straw as it hung over his forehead.

The train whistle blew a sharp, "Woo! Woo!" Then the train started down the little track. It passed buildings that looked familiar to Edison. These were models of places where he once lived and worked. They had been built to honor him. The train itself was a model of the one that had gone from Port Huron to Detroit.

Edison looked out the window. "I can't believe it!" he said, smiling. His eyes had tears of joy.

Suddenly a small boy came into the car. "Candy, apples, newspapers, sandwiches," the boy cried. He sounded the way Edison himself had sounded seventy years before.

The train and the model buildings were part of Greenfield Village in Michigan. The village was built in 1929.

That was the year of a big celebration. It was the fiftieth birthday of the electric light. The celebration was called a Golden Jubilee of Light.

The Edisons came early. They first visited a building that looked like Edison's old laboratory in Newark.

Inside the building Edison saw models of many of his inventions. There was not enough room for all of them. In his lifetime Edison had made more than *one thousand* inventions!

At the end of the Jubilee, a banquet was held in Edison's honor. Five hundred guests were there. Famous men gave speeches about Edison. Some of them said he was a genius. Others called him a miracle maker.

Edison could not hear what they said.

But he could "read" their lips. Mrs. Edison helped him understand. She tapped on his hands in Morse code.

After the speeches, Edison was handed a light bulb. It looked like the first one he had made, fifty years before. Carefully he connected it to the electric power. Everyone in the room was quiet as he slowly pulled the switch.

"It works!" he said to himself, as the light came on. "I always knew it would."